ALL ABOUT DINOSAURS

VELOCIRAPTOR

BookLife

by

Mike Clark

KU-160-686

©2018
Book Life
King's Lynn
Norfolk PE30 4LS

ISBN: 978-1-78637-180-5

All rights reserved
Printed in Malaysia

Written by:
Mike Clark

Edited by:
Charlie Ogden

Designed by:
Matt Rumbelow

A catalogue record for this book
is available from the British Library.

PHOTO CREDITS

Abbreviations: l-left, r-right, b-bottom, t-top, c-centre, m-middle.
Front Cover – Herschel Hoffmeyer. Throughout book: rocks – Nonchanon; leaves – ecco. P1: bg – wawritto. P2-3: bg –
CHALITSA HONGTONG; bl – Herschel Hoffmeyer. P4-5: bg – sergeisimonov; bl – Warpaint. P6-7: bg – Iakov Kalinin; m
– Herschel Hoffmeyer; r – Herschel Hoffmeyer. P8: bg – kaesunza; l – MarcelClemens; m – guysal; r – Ben Townsend/
Wikipedia. P10-11: bg – dugdax; t – Sofia Santos; b – Michael Rosskothen. 12: bg – Windofchange64; 12l – Herschel
Hoffmeyer; 12r – veleknez; 13 – mj007. P14-15: bg – Willequet Manuel; r – Herschel Hoffmeyer. P16-17: bg – . P16: l – PipT;
r – Herschel Hoffmeyer. P17: l – Herschel Hoffmeyer; r – Warpaint. P18-19: bg – i am way. P18: l – Valentyna Chukhlyebova; r –
Herschel Hoffmeyer. P19: r – Herschel Hoffmeyer. P20: bg – Luis Molinero; front – Herschel Hoffmeyer. 21 – cobalt/Wikipedia.
24 – Warpaint. Images are courtesy of Shutterstock.com. With thanks to Getty Images, Thinkstock Photo and iStockphoto.

CONTENTS

Words that appear like this can be found in the glossary on page 23.

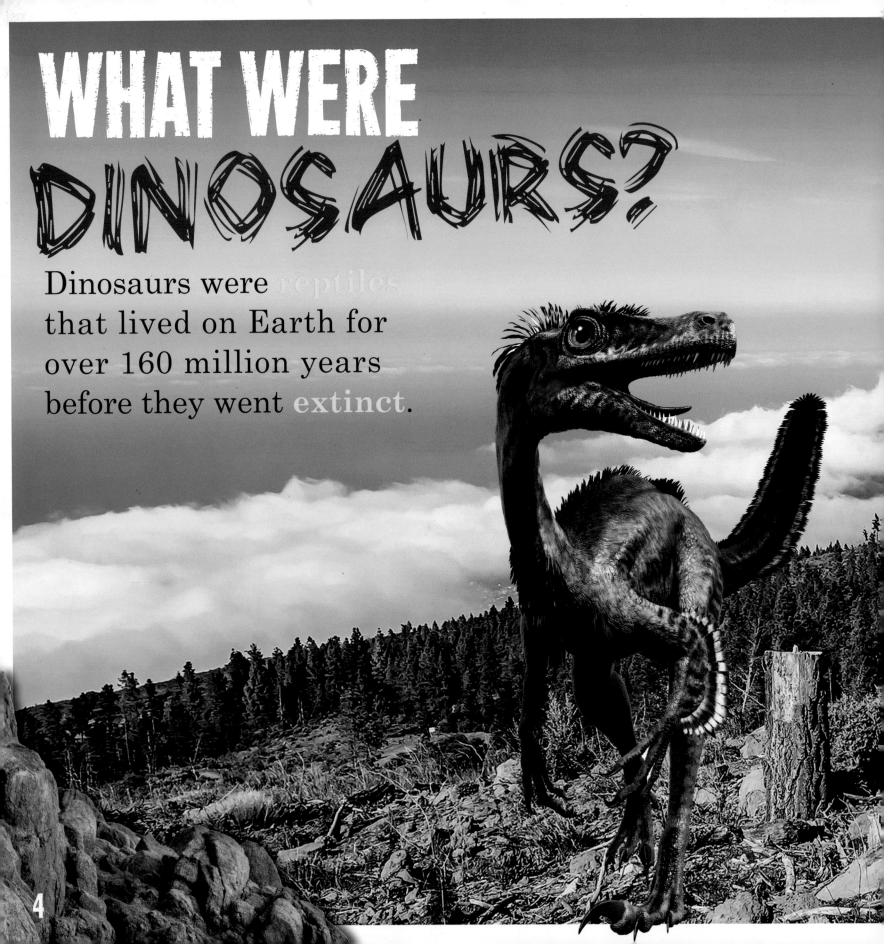

WHAT WERE DINOSAURS?

Dinosaurs were reptiles that lived on Earth for over 160 million years before they went **extinct**.

There were many different types of dinosaur. They lived both on land and in water – and some could even fly!

WHEN WERE DINOSAURS ALIVE?

Dinosaurs first lived around 230 million years ago during a period of time called the Mesozoic period. The last dinosaurs went extinct around 65 million years before humans were alive.

PANGEA

EURASIA

NORTH AMERICA

PACIFIC

SOUTH AMERICA

AFRICA

PACIFIC

INDIA

ANTARTICA

Millions of years ago, all the land on Earth was together in one piece. But during the time of the dinosaurs, it slowly broke up into the different continents that we know today.

WHEN ALL THE LAND ON EARTH WAS TOGETHER IN ONE PIECE, IT WAS CALLED PANGEA.

HOW DO WE KNOW ...?

We know so much about dinosaurs thanks to the scientists, called palaeontologists (pay-lee-on-tol-uh-gists), who study them. They dig up fossils of dinosaurs to find out more about them.

EGG

FOSSIL

Scientists put together the bones they find to try to make full dinosaur skeletons. From these skeletons, scientists can often work out the size and weight of a dinosaur. We can also find out information about what it ate from fossilised food and poo.

SCIENTISTS HAVE EVEN FOUND FOSSILISED EGGS AND FOOTPRINTS BELONGING TO DINOSAURS.

VELOCIRAPTOR SKELETON

VELOCIRAPTOR

The Velociraptor was very small, but it was still a deadly **predator**. It was very fast and hunted animals with its sharp claws and teeth.

NAME	Velociraptor (veh-loss -ih-rap-tor)
LENGTH	2.07 metres
HEIGHT	0.5 metres
WEIGHT	15 kilograms
FOOD	CARNIVORE
WHEN IT LIVED	70–85 million years ago
HOW IT MOVED	Walked on two legs
WEAPONS	Sharp claws and 28 teeth

The Velociraptor went extinct about 70 million years ago. It is believed that they were once birds and could fly. However, over the years they lost the ability to fly and began living on the ground.

SAUROLOPHUS

VELOCIRAPTOR

THE NAME VELOCIRAPTOR MEANS 'SPEEDY THIEF'.

WHAT DID THE  VELOCIRAPTOR LOOK LIKE?

The Velociraptor was about the same size as a small turkey and grew no bigger than two metres long. For many years, it was believed that the Velociraptor had scales, but many palaeontologists now believe it had feathers.

FEATHERS

The Velociraptor's main hunting weapon was its big claws. It had one on each of its back feet. These huge claws were used to grab and hold onto its **prey**.

VELOCIRAPTOR CLAW

THE VELOCIRAPTOR COULD RUN AS FAST AS 60 KILOMETRES PER HOUR – THAT'S AS FAST AS A CAR!

WHERE DID THE VELOCIRAPTOR LIVE?

Velociraptor fossils have only been found in Mongolia. Palaeontologists have studied the places where the fossils have been found and believe that Velociraptors must have liked very warm places.

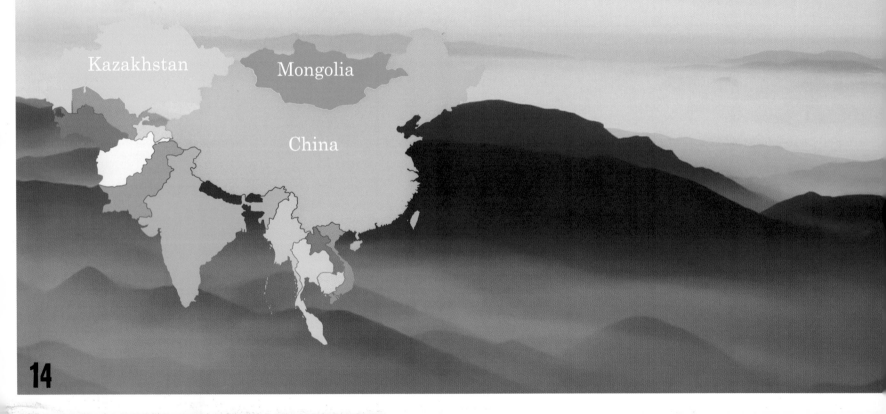

Velociraptors may have lived in groups called packs. This belief is based on the fact that other dinosaurs are known to have lived in packs. However, there are still no fossils that prove that Velociraptors lived in packs.

WHAT DID THE VELOCIRAPTOR EAT?

The Velociraptor was a carnivore. It was very quick and could catch fast-moving prey. It mostly ate small dinosaurs that lived in grasslands and deserts.

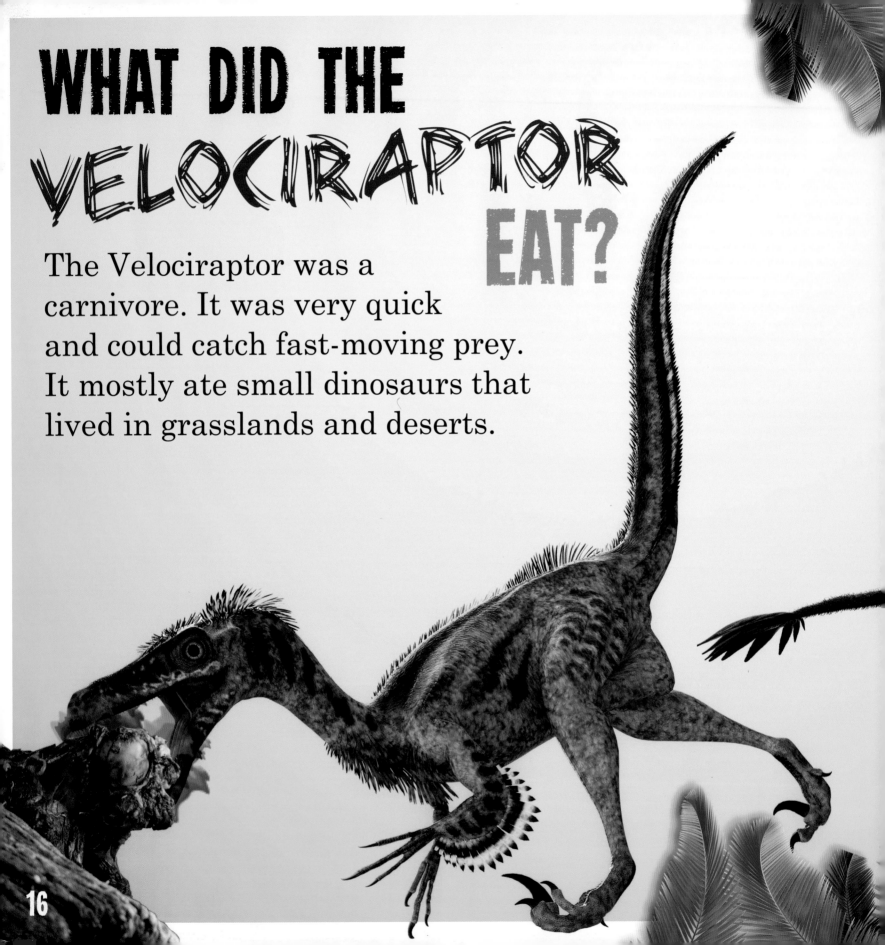

Velociraptors brought down their prey with their huge claws. Palaeontologists believe that the Velociraptor might have also hunted larger dinosaurs such s the Protoceratops (pro-toe-sair-uh-tops). Most Palaeontologists agree that the Protoceratops was the Velociraptor's favourite meal.

WAS THE VELOCIRAPTOR THE FASTEST HUNTER?

Velociraptors could run at up to 60 kilometres per hour when hunting. They could run as fast as many other types of raptor, even though lots of them were much bigger.

UTAHRAPTOR

VELOCIRAPTOR

The Utahraptor (U-tah-rap-tor) could grow to be seven metres long and up to four metres tall. Despite being so big, the Utahraptor ran at the same speed as the Velociraptor.

UTAHRAPTOR

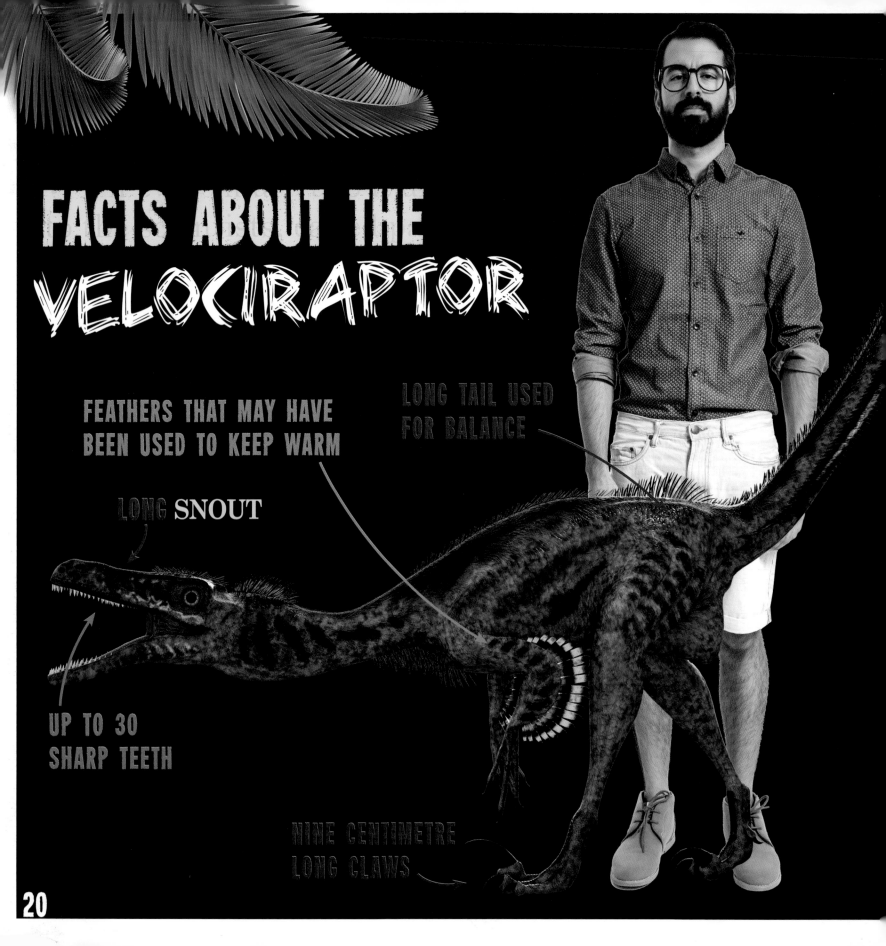

FACTS ABOUT THE VELOCIRAPTOR

FEATHERS THAT MAY HAVE BEEN USED TO KEEP WARM

LONG TAIL USED FOR BALANCE

LONG SNOUT

UP TO 30 SHARP TEETH

NINE CENTIMETRE LONG CLAWS

A VELOCIRAPTOR SKELETON AND A PROTOCERATOPS SKELETON HAVE BEEN FOUND LOCKED IN A BATTLE.

THE PROTOCERATOPS HAS THE VELOCIRAPTOR IN ITS MOUTH.

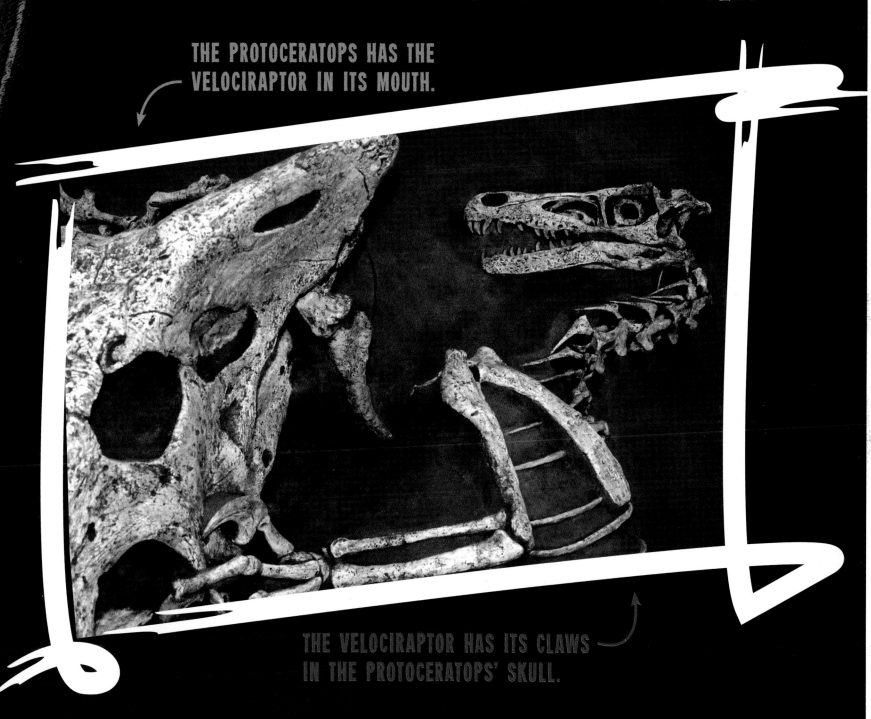

THE VELOCIRAPTOR HAS ITS CLAWS IN THE PROTOCERATOPS' SKULL.

FIND THE VELOCIRAPTOR'S TWIN

FIND MY TWIN!

22

GLOSSARY

carnivore   an animal that eats other animals rather than plants

continents   very large areas of land that are made up of many countries, like Africa and Europe

extinct   a word that describes a species of animal that is no longer alive

fossils   the remains of very old plants and animals that lived a long time ago

Mesozoic   the period of time when dinosaurs lived

predator   an animal that hunts other animals for food

prey   animals that are hunted by other animals for food

reptiles   cold-blooded animals with scales

snout   a type of nose and mouth that sticks out in front of an animal's face

INDEX